# THE GOD
# OF ALL COMFORT

## NORMAN R PERRY

*Other books by N. R. Perry*

THE CRUCIFIED CONQUEROR     80p

IN HIS PRESENCE *(for the bereaved)*     30p

HE KNOWS *(for the sick and suffering)*     30p

85306 1734

*1969 15,000 First Edition*

*1974 15,000 Second Edition*

© *Text Hughes & Coleman Ltd*

© *Illustrations Jarrold & Sons Ltd, Norwich*

*Published by Hughes & Coleman Ltd*

*Printed in Great Britain by Jarrold & Sons Ltd, Norwich*

To my wife
Whose patience, loyalty and love
have made her a true help-meet.

# ACKNOWLEDGEMENTS

It is impossible to produce the most modest book without owing something to the writers of former days whose work in prose and poetry has enriched us all.

To name every individual whose genius has so greatly contributed to our literary treasures is quite impossible. This, however, does not lessen our gratitude to them, and I freely acknowledge my own indebtedness to their work.

I would especially thank among others, the Hutchinson Publishing Group for the use of verses from 'The Poets and Poetry of the Century', edited by A. H. Miles; and to Frederick Warne and Co, Ltd for verses from 'Christian Lyrics'.

NORMAN R. PERRY

# CONTENTS

# INTRODUCTION

The children of God in every age have often felt the need of real comfort. The opposition of unbelievers has discouraged them; the strong and subtle attacks of Satan have disabled them; a sense of failure has depressed them; their besetting sins have disturbed them; the loss of loved ones has distressed them. These things force the believer to cry to God for help and comfort, and we can rejoice that these are available in our times of need.

Reflect prayerfully upon Paul's words in 2 Corinthians 1 : 3, 4, '*Blessed be God, even the Father of our Lord Jesus Christ, the Father of mercies, and the God of all comfort; who comforteth us in all our tribulations, that we may be able to comfort them which are in any trouble, by the comfort wherewith we ourselves are comforted of God.*' Here, the source of comfort is revealed, and here, a testimony to comfort is received.

This little book is an attempt to show how fully God is able to comfort His people in all kinds of trouble. I ask you to follow out the themes dealt with here, in dependence upon the Holy Spirit, and with constant reference to the Scriptures. This will reveal greater riches and profounder depths than can possibly be set out in the small compass of this volume.

7

Highland Burn, Glen More

# THE COMFORT OF GOD'S GRACE

*'For by grace are ye saved through faith; and that not of yourselves: it is the gift of God, not of works, lest any man should boast.'*
Ephesians 2:8, 9.

Some people are inclined to smile whenever Noah or the ark which he built is mentioned. Those, however, who believe the Scriptures to be God's revelation to men, regard Noah and his family as the sole human survivors from the greatest catastrophe and most severe judgement ever visited upon the earth—this family alone being miraculously preserved by God Himself. In Genesis 6:8 we have the word 'grace' first mentioned, *'But Noah found grace in the eyes of the Lord.'*

Grace may briefly be defined as God's unmerited favour—His undeserved kindness towards us, and is in every way consistent with His revealed character. As a result of this, it is certain that He will not act graciously towards us one day and ungraciously the next. It is in the nature of man to change, but it is not in God's nature, for He has declared, 'I change not'. What a blessed word this is in a world of change and uncertainty. If we have received the call by grace through the Gospel of Jesus Christ, we may often find God's dealings with us very strange, but they will never be ungracious. When God calls a person by His grace it is in harmony with His own mighty purpose of salvation; and so great is His grace, so strong is His hand, that Jesus said concerning God's chosen ones, *'No man is able to pluck them out of my Father's hand.'* (John 10:29).

How clearly the Scriptures teach that it is God who acts first in the work of salvation, as Paul declares in Galatians 1:15 *'. . . God . . . called me by His grace. . . .'* Thus God is seen in the initial stage of the work of grace; and the poet rightly sings

> *Grace first inscribed my name*
> *In God's eternal book. . .*

9

As it is not in God's nature to commence something and then abandon it, we are not surprised to find that Paul, when acutely conscious of weakness and insufficiency, was spoken to by God Himself in these words, '*My grace is sufficient for thee....*' (2 Corinthians 12:9) Thus neither

> *Grief nor pain, nor any sorrow*
> *Rends thy heart to Him unknown,*
> *He today, and He tomorrow*
> *Grace sufficient gives His own.*
> T. Mackellar

The tried and troubled saints in every age have proved the sufficiency of God's grace, as one, writing hundreds of years after Paul, testified:

> *And new supplies each hour I meet*
> *While pressing on to God.*

In that great resurrection chapter, 1 Corinthians 15:10, we have Paul's ringing testimony, '*But by the grace of God I am what I am; and His grace which was bestowed upon me was not in vain; but I laboured more abundantly than they all: yet not I, but the grace of God which was with me.*'

The fact that God's people have to undergo chastening and endure tribulations, is no evidence that God has ceased to be gracious, history shows that many of God's choicest saints have been called to greatest suffering. As Samuel Rutherford faced death, he used words like these:

> *The bride eyes not her garment,*
> *But her dear bridegroom's face;*
> *I will not gaze at glory,*
> *But on my King of Grace.*

For you and me to know that our present safety and future security depends, not on our poor weak efforts, but on a God whose grace abounds towards us, is a sure stay in times of trouble. To be assured that God's grace is effectual in its call, is sufficient in its continual supply, and that it will be supreme in its consummation, is most comforting knowledge. This certainty is reflected in the lines:

> *'Twas grace that kept me to this day,*
> *And will not let me go.*

In the 1st Epistle of Peter, chapter 5, verse 10, we read, *'But the God of all grace, who hath called us unto His eternal glory by Christ Jesus, after that ye have suffered a while, make you perfect, stablish, strengthen, settle you.'* Here surely the purposes and processes of God's grace are clearly revealed, and how blessedly they accord with the words in the 84th Psalm where at verse 11 we read, *'The Lord will give grace and glory. . . .'* This is the Divine order and both are sure. If we possess the first, the second must follow, for they are inseparable.

> *Grace is glory in the bud,*
> *and glory is grace at the full.*
> T. Brooks

Reflect often then, on the wonder of God's grace to sinful man; for 'it bringeth salvation'; seek too, the aid of the Holy Spirit as you read His gracious words of hope, peace and joy. Thus will you learn more of what it means to be comforted by the grace of that God who remains unchangeably gracious.

# THE COMFORT OF GOD'S MERCY

*'And the publican, standing afar off, would not lift up so much as his eyes unto heaven, but smote upon his breast, saying, God be merciful to me a sinner.'*

Luke 18 : 13.

Here we have a picture of a man in dire distress of soul. From the human standpoint he is a pitiable spectacle. Compared with the Pharisee, whose prayer had preceded his, he is a picture of dejection. His prayer consists only of a description of himself, and a plea for mercy. It is simple, brief, and direct. He stands afar off—apart from the altar. The Pharisee and the publican are contrasted thus by Crawshaw:

> *One stands up close and treads on high,*
> *Where the other dare not bend his eye.*
> *One nearer to God's altar trod,*
> *The other to the altar's God.*

Take comfort, you who feel you can only stand as a sinner before God. Observe that the poor publican cried to God for mercy, and was assured of justification. The Pharisee proudly claimed that he was not unjust; the Publican was said by Christ to be justified. How many since then, when under conviction of sin, have cried out in agony of soul for mercy. Not only publicans, but kings, have cried thus. Listen to David's broken-hearted cry, as recorded in Psalm 51 : 1. *'Have mercy upon me, O God, according to thy loving kindness: according unto the multitude of Thy tender mercies blot out my transgressions.'* Great and grievous sin had clouded his spiritual vision, and dissipated his joy. He was acutely and painfully aware of the holiness of God and the enormity of his guilt. When this had been brought home to him, then he cried for mercy: one of the greatest comforts that the child of God can know, is that, *'His mercy endureth for ever'*. (Psalm 136).

How often, when conscious of having offended a holy

13

Pistyll Rhaiadr Falls, Montgomeryshire

God, and merited His just punishment, has the sinful soul cried out with Habakkuk, 'In wrath remember mercy.' If, like the Publican, your consciousness of guilt is so great and overpowering that you feel afraid even to call to God for help, take courage, for while

> *"Broken hearts and downcast eyes,*
> *Dare not lift themselves to Thee,*
> *Yet Thou canst interpret sighs:*
> *'God be merciful to me.'"*

Reading the experiences of many of God's saints, one has so often been struck with the fact that at times they were almost overwhelmed with the realisation that in their own estimation and feelings they were poor sinners, weak sinners, great sinners, lost sinners, vile sinners; and it may be that you, too, know this experience.

Then blessedly, sweetly and with great relief, has come the assurance that 'the mercy of the Lord is from everlasting to everlasting', and with joy and praise in the heart, one has exclaimed with James Ormiston:

> *Lord, how tender is Thy mercy,*
> *Free as tender, rich as free;*
> *Pitying, pardoning chief of sinners*
> *Pitying, pardoning even me.*

It was the simple, thankful testimony of the Apostle Paul that '*I obtained mercy. . . .*' (1 Timothy 1 : 13).

How true it is that the wonder of God's mercy is only appreciated when we realise the appalling 'sinfulness of sin'. It is seen to the full at the Cross, and its effect can be measured by the mighty sacrifice of Christ there.

> *"Thy mercy in Jesus*
> *Exempts me from hell;*
> *Its glories I'll sing*
> *And its wonders I'll tell;*
> *'Twas Jesus my Friend,*
> *When He hung on the tree*
> *Who opened the channel*
> *Of mercy for me."*

14

Lochan na Achlaise, Argyll

The only ground of hope for the sinner is the mercy of God, revealed in Jesus Christ, who always during His earthly life responded to the cry for mercy. So it was in Old Testament days; for see how God made provision in the tabernacle (Exodus 25 : 17–22), saying, '*And thou shalt put the mercy seat above upon the ark . . . and there I will meet with thee. . . .*' As it was then, so now it is still true that:

> *From every stormy wind that blows,*
> *From every swelling tide of woes,*
> *There is a calm, a safe retreat,*
> '*Tis found beneath the mercy-seat.*
> Stowell

Ponder then the statement in Ephesians 2 : 4, '*God . . . is rich in mercy*', and present yourself as a poor needy sinner at His door of mercy, and you will, in the realisation of mercy granted, be comforted of God.

# THE COMFORT OF GOD'S LOVE

*For I am persuaded, that neither death nor life, nor angels, nor principalities, nor powers, nor things present, nor things to come, nor height, nor depth, nor any other creature, shall be able to separate us from the love of God, which is in Christ Jesus our Lord.*

Romans 8:38, 39

What wonderful words these are, calculated to stimulate the trembling heart of the most fearful saint, and to console the most downcast believer. The love of God is something which no man can measure; so many assurances of God's love to His people are given in the Scriptures, and such clear evidence of it revealed at the Cross, that it is amazing that we should ever doubt it. Consider the Lord's words given in Jeremiah 31:3, '*Yea I have loved thee with an everlasting love: therefore with loving kindness have I drawn thee.*'

> *His love, what mortal thought can reach,*
> *What mortal tongue display?*
> *Imaginations utmost stretch*
> *In wonder dies away!*
>
> Steele

How happy are they to whom God has once revealed His love; who can say with Paul, 'He loved me . . .'; for this love is a personal love, indicated by Christ's words in John 16, v. 27, '*For the Father Himself loveth you. . . .*' It remains true however, that there are times when the Christian is not as conscious of the love of God, as he would like to be. There is a coldness and a deadness, which causes him great searching of heart and real distress of soul, for to man's dim sight:

> *The truths of love are like the sea*
> *For clearness and for mystery.*
>
> Patmore

Let such a troubled one be helped by the remembrance that he could not feel the lack of something he had never before felt or experienced.

17

Ashness Bridge, Cumberland

*Think not of what is from thee kept;*
*Think, rather, what thou hast received:*
*Thine eyes have smiled, if they have wept;*
*Thy heart has danced, if it has grieved.*
*Rich comforts yet shall be thine own;*
*Yea, God Himself shall wipe thine eyes;*
*And still His love alike is shown*
*In what He gives, and what denies.*

Henry S. Sutton

All God's people know something of walking in the shadows, but they can be confident that this does not mean that God has withdrawn His love from them. God is love; and all His dealings with His people are in love. Perhaps Rutherford's experience will help to explain why the love of God is not always felt in the heart:

*But flowers need night's cool darkness,*
*The moonlight and the dew;*
*So Christ from one who loved it,*
*His shining oft withdrew . . .*

Listen also to Charles Wesley:

*God only knows the love of God;*
*O that it now were shed abroad*
*In this poor stony heart!*
*For love I sigh; for love I pine,*
*This only portion, Lord be mine,*
*Be mine this better part!*

Thus the saints of former days expressed themselves, evidencing the same changes and fluctuations as we know today. Those who have felt 'the love of God shed abroad in their hearts', must remember that He who so loved, that He sent His own Son to die for them, may sometimes find it necessary to discipline them. This does not mean that He has deserted them. Far from it. This is an impossibility, for

*Whom once He loves, He never leaves*
*But loves them to the end.*

18

The Apostle John in 1 John 3:1, writes, '*Behold what manner of love the Father has bestowed upon us, that we should be called the Sons of God....*' Yes, 'Sons of God', but not always the obedient children we should be; therefore we must expect to find such a passage as Hebrews 12:5, 6, '*My son, despise not thou the chastening of the Lord, nor faint when thou art rebuked of Him: for whom the Lord loveth, He chasteneth, and scourgeth every son whom He receiveth....*' How much, and how often, we need the chastening hand of our God, but how sure we may be that it is always a loving hand. Sometimes we feel the soothing, calming, and loving touch of His hand, and we rejoice. Yet

> *Even when He chideth*
> *Tender is His tone.*

The child of God, meditating upon the love of God, will surely prove that Cowper's words are blessedly true:

> *Mine is an unchanging love,*
> *Higher than the heights above;*
> *Deeper than the depths beneath,*
> *Free and faithful, strong as death.*

So in the contemplation of an unfathomable and unchanging love, the believer is comforted of God.

# THE COMFORT OF GOD'S HOLINESS

'*For thus saith the high and lofty One that inhabiteth eternity, whose name is Holy: I dwell in the high and holy place, with him also that is of a contrite and humble spirit, to revive the spirit of the humble, and to revive the heart of the contrite ones.*'

Isaiah 57:15.

What mortal mind can grasp the wonder of this grand utterance, or what pen can do justice to such breathtaking words? How can sinful man possibly imagine a Being of absolute Holiness in any sense condescending to have dealings with him? In what way can man draw any comfort from the Holiness of God?

Clearly, man cannot approach unto God with any hope of acceptance on the ground of personal holiness; for he is everywhere in Scripture seen as, and said to be, a sinner, and unholy in God's sight; and he knows this to be true. Isaiah's vision of the seraphim, and the awe-inspiring words that he heard them utter, '*Holy, holy, holy, is the Lord of Hosts . . .*' (Isaiah 6:3), drew from him the cry, 'Woe is me.' All the saints of God have been overwhelmed by the thought of the absolute holiness of God, and in various ways have sought to express their feelings in view of it; as for example Heber, when he wrote

> *Holy, holy, holy! though the darkness hide Thee,*
> *Though the eye of sinful man Thy glory may not see;*
> *Only Thou art holy: there is none beside Thee,*
> *Perfect in power, in love, and purity.*

The contrast is represented by the lines of Thomas Binney, and the problems thrown into bold relief, as he asks

> *Oh! how shall I, whose native sphere*
> *Is dark, whose mind is dim,*
> *Before the Ineffable appear,*
> *And on my naked spirit bear*
> *The uncreated beam?*

21

Beresford Dale, Derbyshire

How? This is the great question, and it is posed in Job 9:2. *'How should a man be just with God?'* As God cannot change, He must ever remain Holy and Just. He cannot act unjustly, nor ever cease to be Holy. Nothing that He says or does, can or will, in any way violate His Holiness. If therefore there is any word of hope, or any way of salvation proposed by Him, we may be absolutely sure that it will accord in every detail with the demands of His holiness. The comfort that the Christian has in the contemplation of God's holiness must derive from the fact that no plan of salvation prepared, executed, and revealed by Him, would in any way conflict with that holiness.

In other words, if there is any way possible by which man can hope to stand uncondemned and unashamed in the presence of a holy God, then that way must completely satisfy the demands of this Holy One Himself. Let another verse from a hymn already quoted, speak for us here:

> *There is a way for man to rise*
> *To that sublime abode,*
> *An offering and a sacrifice,*
> *A Holy Spirit's energies,*
> *An Advocate with God.*

God's way of salvation is by faith in Jesus Christ, Who 'bore our sins in His own body on the tree. . . .' Jesus Christ came from heaven to do this mighty work, which none other could do. He did it to the absolute satisfaction of His Holy Father, who declared Himself well pleased with all that His Son had done.

Listen to the words recorded in Revelation 7:14–17. *'These are they which came out of great tribulation, and have washed their robes, and made them white in the blood of the Lamb. Therefore are they before the Throne of God . . . and God shall wipe away all tears from their eyes.'* See where these people are, 'Before the Throne of God'. See why they are there—because they are 'washed in the blood

River Avon, Stratford-upon-Avon

of the Lamb'. If the Holy God is satisfied with what Christ has done for the believer, and in the believer, then all must be well, and we can draw great comfort from the fact that God the Holy One, has made it possible for

*The sons of ignorance and night*
*To dwell in the Eternal Light*
*Through the Eternal Love.*

Psalm 89:35, declares, '*Once have I sworn by my holiness that I will not lie unto David.*' The Holy God is a God Who cannot lie, because He is Holy. Therefore the child of God having received the promise of life and adoption from a thrice Holy God, can, in meditating upon such a being, be comforted because He is Holy.

# THE COMFORT OF GOD'S WORD

*'For ever, O Lord, Thy Word is settled in heaven.'*

Psalm 119:89.

*'I hope in Thy Word.'*

Psalm 119:114.

*'The Word of the Lord endureth for ever.'*

1 Peter 1:25.

The child of God has not been left to grope his way unaided through the years of his earthly pilgrimage. God has graciously inspired and preserved a book, which, besides revealing the mind and will of God, serves as a guide and chart to the believer as he journeys on. This book is known to us as the Bible; it is to this book we must go for instruction and help, for it is the only book which bears the insignia of the Deity. No other book can compare with it; he who holds in his hand the Bible, the Word of God, holds a most precious thing.

Upon the statements of this Book millions have trusted themselves completely. Because of their faith in this Book men and women have laid down their lives, and many are suffering today for the same reason. We are not making any attempt here to prove the truth of this Book. It is assumed that the reader is already convinced of this. It is desired rather to emphasise that in this book is to be discovered the source of true comfort, as is stated in Romans 15:4, *'For whatsoever things were written aforetime, were written for our learning, that we through patience and comfort of the scripture might have hope.'* Here is revealed the majesty, might, and mercy of God. How wonderfully true it is, as the poet Cowper so beautifully expresses it.

> *A glory gilds the sacred page,*
> *Majestic, like the sun;*
> *It gives a light to every age;*
> *It gives, but borrows none.*

25

Crathie Church, Deeside

The sinner coming to this book, will find it disturbing; for it does not mince words concerning him and his doom, if he persists in his sinful way. At the same time it shows him the only way of salvation. The saint, whether he be a scholar or a man without any pretensions to scholarship, will find here, words to suit his need. It is, in the words of Gregory the Great—'A stream where alike the elephant may swim and the lamb may wade.' There is no condition into which a man may come, where he will find the Bible irrelevant. As human nature remains unchanged, so this unchanging Book has the answer to his need.

> *Christ said not to His first conventicle,*
> *Go forth and preach impostures to the world;*
> *But gave them Truth to build on; and the sound*
> *Was mighty on their lips;*

Dante

In the book of Daniel, the Word of God is called '*the scripture of truth*' (Chapter 10:21); and in John 10:35, Christ declared, '*. . . the scripture cannot be broken.*' How we ought to rejoice in the fact that we have such a book and that we have liberty to read it. Consider how great men of the past have revelled in it; for example Milton, who wrote, 'There are no songs comparable to the Songs of Zion; no orations equal to those of the Prophets; and no politics like those which the Scriptures teach.' Or take Selden's words, 'There is no book upon which we can rest in a dying moment but the Bible.' Richard Pollok, in his 'Course of Time' writes thus:

> *Most wondrous book, bright candle of the Lord!*
> *Star of eternity! the only star*
> *By which the barque of man can navigate*
> *The sea of life, and gain the coast of bliss*
> *Securely . . .*

Or note how Locke expresses his feelings concerning this book. 'It has God for its author, salvation for its end, and truth without any mixture of error, for its matter: it is all pure, all sincere, nothing too much, nothing wanting.' Such tributes could be multiplied, and they could be drawn today from all parts of the world, and from every strata of society.

Here in this book, is to be found real comfort, for the despondent, the weary, the bereaved, the disappointed, the discouraged. It comforts the saint who has back-slidden, and speaks of One who restoreth the soul. In face of the tremendous problems which rear their heads so menacingly, it speaks of God who is over all, Omnipotent.

It gives assurance of strength for the weak, guidance for the perplexed, hope for the hopeless, and forgiveness for the sinner through 'the blood of the Cross'.

Here the blessed Redeemer's voice is heard saying, 'Let not your heart be troubled'. O that we might read prayerfully, with opened eyes and receptive hearts, the unchanging Word of God.

*Lord grant us all aright to learn*
*The wisdom it imparts;*
*And to its heavenly teachings turn*
*With simple childlike hearts.*

Barton

Consider this wondrous book, note its stability in an unstable world, take its utterances as coming from God Himself, and you will find in your soul the increasing comfort of the Word, by which you are comforted of God.

# THE COMFORT OF GOD'S PRESENCE

*'My presence shall go with thee and I will give thee rest.'*

Exodus 33 : 14.

Moses had said to God, 'See Thou sayest unto me, Bring up this people: and thou hast not let me know whom Thou wilt send with me. . . .' The passage quoted at the top of this page was God's reply, and what a reply it was.

In the desert of Midian, God had said to Moses, before he went in to Pharoah, 'Certainly I will be with thee.' Moses had seen the fulfilment of these words; and the magicians of Egypt had been forced to acknowledge, when they failed to match the miracles wrought by God through Moses, 'This is the finger of God.' Practical proof was thus given, both to Moses, and to Egypt, of a super-natural power at work among them.

When Joshua was called to succeed Moses, he was assured twice over by the words, *'As I was with Moses, so I will be with thee.'* (Joshua 1 : 5). Yet it remains a matter for wonder and amazement that God, the Eternal, Almighty, Holy God, should in any way be present where man, His sinful creature is. This wonder is surely reflected in Solomon's words at the dedication of the temple, when he asked, *'But will God indeed dwell on the earth? Behold, the heaven and heaven of heavens cannot contain Thee; how much less this house that I have builded?'* (1 Kings 8 : 27).

In view of the solemn fact of God's omnipresence as revealed in Psalm 139, we must approach the thought of God and His presence with men, in a spirit of awe and worship; for the presence of God can be devastating, as His enemies have always found, or delightful, as His saints know to their joy. What more simple or sublime passage could be found than Genesis 5 : 24, *'And Enoch walked with God: and he was not, for God took him.'* Alexander Grosart has expressed in later years what Enoch proved so long ago:

29

Rock-climbing, Borrowdale, Cumberland

*No one so far away as God,*
  *Yet none who is so near*
*Eternity is His abode;*
  *But lo! I find Him here;*
*Within my heart—that by His grace*
*He chosen has for dwelling place.*

This is the thought we would emphasise, not so much the fact of God's Omni-presence, not the fact alone that He is everywhere present, and in supreme control of the whole universe, but that He is with men as a friend and helper. If any should feel that this borders on the presumptuous, let it be borne in mind that Jesus said, 'Where two or three are gathered together in my name, there am I in the midst of them.' It is this personal realisation of God's presence that brings joy and peace to the believer.

Though the universe is so vast, and the world sometimes so cold, to feel that there is one who can draw near, as Christ drew near to His disciples, will dispel the sense of loneliness which can so depress the Spirit. It is not for relics or representations that God's children long. This thought is finely expressed in the lines of Elizabeth Charles, from her poem, 'Never further than Thy Cross!' We quote just two verses:

*Of no fond relics, sadly dear,*
  *O Master! are Thine own possest;*
*The crown of thorns, the cross, the spear,*
  *The purple robe, the seamless vest.*

*Nay, relics are for those who mourn*
  *The memory of an absent friend;*
*Not absent Thou, nor we forlorn!*
  *With you each day until the end!*

Yes, indeed, Jesus said, '*Lo I am with you alway, even unto the end of the world.*' (Matthew 28:20).

How many can bear glad testimony to the fact of God's presence to comfort, and of help received in times of need; as Paul, when awaiting death declared,

'*The Lord stood with me, and strengthened me . . .*' (2 Timothy 4:17).

Or take the sweet words of Samuel Rutherford:

> *Oft in yon sea-beat prison*
> *My Lord and I held tryst.*

How necessary it is that we should be constantly assured of God's gracious presence, and how we need to pray that nothing may come between God and our souls; for this brings sorrow and pain, and we are sadly conscious of the interference. All Christians know what Montgomery meant when he wrote

> *Yet clouds will intervene,*
> *And all my prospect flies!*
> *Like Noah's dove, I flit between*
> *Rough seas and stormy skies.*

Then it is helpful to remember that God's presence unrealised, does not of necessity mean God's presence has been withdrawn; but only that He is hiding His face for some wise purpose. Furthermore, He will reveal Himself again, and speak words of peace and re-assurance, when the soul will say with renewed joy,

> *Then, then I feel that He,*
> *(Remembered or forgot),*
> *The Lord, is never far from me,*
> *Though I perceive Him not.*

Further, the believer has the assurance, 'I will never leave thee nor forsake thee.'

> *Fear not, I am with thee, oh be not dismayed!*
> *I, I am thy God, and will still give thee aid:*
> *I'll strengthen thee, help thee, and cause thee to stand.*
> *Upheld by My righteous omnipotent hand.*

God does not deal with His people by remote control; no rather, He is '*a very present help in trouble*'. (Psalm 46:1).

May the sweet warmth of the Divine presence frequently remind us that we are being comforted of God.

# THE COMFORT OF GOD'S POWER

*'Hast thou not known? hast thou not heard, that the everlasting God, the Lord, the Creator of the ends of the earth, fainteth not, neither is weary? There is no searching of His understanding. He giveth power to the faint. . . .'*

Isaiah 40:28–29.

When we speak of the power of man, or the power of nature, we must always remember that these are relative terms. For example, the power of a child is small compared with that of a grown man. The first thing then, to be borne in mind when we speak of the power of God, is that it is not relative, but Absolute. Because of this, we have such questions as, *'To whom then will ye liken me, or shall I be equal, saith the Holy One?'* (Isaiah 40:25). Or in Job 40:9, *'Hast thou an arm like God?'* Or again, Psalm 62:11. *'Power belongeth unto God.'* Such examples could be multiplied from Scripture.

In days when man's achievements are paraded before us, it behoves us to consider that when put beside the works of God, they are seen to be infinitesimal. It is true therefore still, and will ever remain true, that, *'the Lord God omnipotent reigneth'*. (Revelation 19:6). There is no sphere in the universe where God's power is not absolute.

> "*The spacious firmament on high,*
> *With all the blue ethereal sky,*
> *The spangled heavens and shining frame,*
> *Their great Original proclaim.*
> *The unwearied sun, from day to day*
> *Does his Creator's power display;*
> *And publishes in every land*
> *The work of an Almighty hand.*"

King Nebuchadnezzar, after his great boasting and subsequent humbling, was compelled to say concerning the Most High, *'. . . None can stay His hand, or say unto Him, What doest Thou?'* (Daniel 4:35).

As in these days we see man performing what to

33

Cliffs of Moher, County Clare

others seem to be super-human feats, and revealing powers of which our ancestors had no knowledge, let us be careful lest we exalt the creature into the position of creator. It is true that there are forces being let loose by man, which are terrifying in their possibilities. This is plain for all to see, and to many it causes great fear. Man is indeed potent, that is, powerful, having great influence and authority; but he is not, nor ever can be Omnipotent, that is, Almighty, possessing unlimited power. Here is the believer's comfort, that there is only One who can say to all other powers, whatever their nature may be, '*Hitherto shalt thou come, but no further: and here shall thy proud waves be stayed!*' (Job 38:11). No threat of devils or men, can affect Him, nor in any way inhibit Him. Consequently, if we have this vision of the Almighty and believe it, we can understand the quiet confidence of the Psalmist when he exclaimed, '*The Lord is on my side; I will not fear; what can man do unto me?*' (Psalm 118:6).

> "*Strive not, nor struggle, thy poor might*
>   *Can never wrest*
> *The meanest thing to serve thy will;*
> *All power is His alone: be still,*
>   *And Trust and Rest.*"

Let your thoughts revolve around some of the mighty manifestations of God's power, as when the angels sang at the Incarnation, when Christ was born. See the suffering Man upon the cross, and listen to the words of Him who suffered there, who, after His resurrection and before He returned to heaven, said 'All power is given unto Me in heaven and in earth. . . .'

Let the mystery of godliness be ever before you, and contemplate the wonder of the fact, that those hands which lifted up the little children, which touched the blind, the deaf, the leprous, which were outstretched upon the tree, and then upraised in blessing before His ascension, are the hands of Deity.

34

Aysgarth, Yorkshire

*Under the shadow of Thy throne*
*Thy saints have dwelt secure:*
*Sufficient is Thine arm alone,*
*And our defence is sure.*

Watts

Seek comfort, where true comfort is to be found, in the Almighty tenderness of Him who controls the stars, caresses the flowers into loveliness, and cradles the saint in His arms. You may depend upon Him, and Him alone, for time and for eternity. John Newton wrote

*He who has help'd me hitherto*
*Will help me all my journey through;*
*And give me daily cause to raise*
*New Ebenezers to His praise.*

He will do this, because He has promised and because, 'He is able'.

Thus, in contemplating Omnipotence, the saint is comforted of God.

# THE COMFORT OF GOD'S PROMISES

*'. . . God that cannot lie, promised . . .'*

Titus 1 : 2.

The value of a promise depends upon the character of the promiser, and his ability to do what he has promised. Thus we know that promises made to us by some people are practically worthless, because we are aware of their character. They are untrustworthy; hence any promise made by them cannot be relied upon. When we come to consider the promises of God, we can at once, and without fear, dismiss from our minds any misgivings on any point.

The simple words quoted above should dispel all doubt concerning God's promises, for He 'cannot lie'. It is not possible for Him to lie. We may, through ignorance, utter words which are not true, or through failure to recognise our limitations, promise what we are unable to carry out. Not so with God. Sometimes He may promise what to man appears an impossible thing, as in the case of Abraham. When God promised him a son, we read that Abraham was, 'fully persuaded, that what He had promised, He was able also to perform'. The faith of Abraham in God's promise was fully justified, as faith in all God's promises is always justified.

> *I trust His righteous character,*
> *His counsel, promise, and His power;*
> *His honour and His Name's at stake,*
> *To save me from the burning lake.*
> E. Mote

Every promise, writes Salter, is built upon four pillars: 'God's justice or holiness, which will not suffer Him to deceive; His grace or goodness, which will not suffer Him to forget; His truth, which will not suffer Him to change; and His power, which makes Him able to accomplish.'

Primroses

The promises of God are described by Peter as, *'exceeding great and precious'*. (2 Peter 1:4). They are great indeed, because of the source from which they come, and precious because of the subjects with which they deal.

> *'All I have is thine,' saith He,*
> *'All things are yours,' He saith again;*
> *All the promises for thee*
> *Are sealed with Jesus Christ's, Amen.*

There is a promise in God's word for every possible situation into which the Christian may be brought. A portrait gallery of men and women who trusted in the promises that God made to them, can be examined at any time by a reference to Hebrews, 11. One thing, however, that must always be kept in mind, is that God's promises are fulfilled in His time, and His way. This often means that we have to wait, and the waiting is not easy; for the naturally impatient heart of man desires to see at once, the fulfilment of the promise. This eleventh chapter of Hebrews shows us that in almost every case, these men and women of old had to wait, as Simeon had to wait, 'for the consolation of Israel'. Miss A. L. Waring expresses this aspect beautifully as she sings

> *Sometimes I long for promised bliss,*
>   *But it will not come too late—*
> *And the songs of patient spirits rise*
>   *From the place wherein I wait;*
> *While in the faith that makes no haste*
>   *My soul has time to see*
> *A kneeling host of Thy redeemed,*
>   *In fellowship with me.*

It may be that you have had a promise applied to your heart, and are still waiting for its fulfilment. We learn from the Word of God, and from the lives of the saints, that God often keeps His people waiting; but of this we may be sure, His word will be fulfilled. He has

Woodland Aconite

never failed one who has trusted in Him, whether the promise on which the soul relied related to providence or grace. To take God at His word is to honour Him. To doubt His faithful promises is to dishonour Him.

He has promised grace; He has promised eternal life; He will never break His word, for He is 'God, who cannot lie'.

*Trust His rich promises of grace,*
*So shall they be fulfilled in thee;*
*God never yet forsook at need*
*The soul that trusted Him indeed.*
                    Lyra Germanica

Happy is he who trusts in God's pledged word at all times, for he will indeed in trusting thus, be comforted of God.

# THE COMFORT OF GOD'S WISDOM

*'O the depth of the riches, both of the wisdom and knowledge of God! how unsearchable are his judgments, and his ways past finding out!*

Romans 11:33.

It is quite evident that there is a Master mind somewhere. We see and admire both wisdom and knowledge among men, but still we know that there is a source from which their wisdom is derived. Here again, the Christian believes that his God is the All-Wise One, and that the wisdom of men is ignorance in the sight of God. The God of the Bible is seen as the God whose wisdom is infinite, and as one who, in consequence, can never be out-witted by man.

Carlyle once wrote, 'The wise man is but a clever infant, spelling letters from a hierographical prophetic book, the lexicon of which lies in eternity.' Such an utterance from such a man as he, should serve to put us in our right place. Yet we all tend to imagine ourselves wiser, or more knowledgeable, than we really are, and have painfully to find out our own abysmal ignorance. The wisdom of man is ever seeking to discover the secrets of the universe, but the more he finds, the more he realises how little he really knows, and how much more there is to find out. So often we have to say:

> *"Around my path life's mysteries*
> *Their deepening shadows throw;*
> *And as I gaze and ponder,*
> *They dark and darker grow."*

Especially is this so when man turns his attention to origins, for he finds himself baffled, and his conclusions are contradictory. When He seeks for a God whom he can understand or trace, he fails: for, as Zophar asked, *'Canst thou by searching find out God?'* (Job 11:7). Or again as Paul declared, *'The world by wisdom knew not God . . . '* (1 Corinthians 1:21). Let the believer know

41

Selworthy

that he can always rest upon the Bible revelation of God, and obtain all the wisdom he needs from Him.

This trust in God, we know, will often bring upon him the ridicule of the world; but what Gregory said, hundreds of years ago, regarding the ministers of the gospel, can well be pondered by all Christians. He wrote, 'The minister of the Gospel must not be afraid of the conflict with the wisdom of the world. God first gathered the unlearned, afterwards philosophers; nor hath He taught fishermen by orators, but He hath subdued orators by fishermen.'

> *The man with earthly wisdom high uplifted*
> *Is in God's sight a fool;*
> *But he in heavenly truth most deeply gifted*
> *Sits lowest in Christ's School.*
>
> J. D. Burns

He who queries the wisdom of God only displays his own ignorance. To rely upon human wit or wisdom, is to lean upon a broken reed. There are so many situations into which we are brought, which are so complex as to leave us utterly bewildered; we have to exclaim with Jehoshaphat, *'Neither know we what to do: but our eyes are upon Thee.'* (2 Chronicles 20:12). This at once reminds us of the words of James, *'If any of you lack wisdom, let him ask of God. . . .'* (James 1:5). With great thankfulness then, we would reflect upon the wisdom of God, not only as displayed in the universe, but as revealed in the Scriptures. Truly we sing,

> *O Word of God Incarnate!*
> *O Wisdom from on high!*
> *O Truth unchanged, unchanging,*
> *O Light of our dark sky;*
>
> W. W. How

What a comfort is found when reflecting upon the wisdom of God, to know that it is He who in infinite wisdom guides us with unerring accuracy and in tender love. Never does He have to seek advice from another;

never does He make a mistake. These are very easy statements to make, but if they are true, as the Christian believes, then they must profoundly affect our thinking, and be of tremendous consolation to us.

Christ's words raised astonishment among the people when He spoke to them; so much so that they asked, '*Whence hath this man this wisdom?*' (Matthew 13:54). While in 1 Corinthians 1:30, we have the glorious assertion '. . . *Christ Jesus . . . of God is made unto us wisdom. . . .*' In Christ are revealed, '. . . *all the treasures of wisdom and knowledge . . .*' (Colossians 2:3). They who know this, cry with Hurn:

*O condescend to teach us here,*
*And be our constant Guide.*

Comforting indeed, is the thought that our God not only has all knowledge, but the wisdom to know how to use it. Happy are they whose lives are fully committed into the hands of an All-Wise God, to whom the great paean of praise is expressed thus, 'To the only wise God our *Saviour* . . .' (Jude 25).

Saviour! Yes indeed; may we never forget that He who is All-Wise is our Saviour; for then we shall not fail, as we reflect upon this theme, to be comforted of God.

# THE COMFORT OF GOD'S GUIDANCE

*'Thou shalt guide me with thy counsel, and afterward receive me to glory.'*

Psalm 73:24.

Such a verse as this assures the child of God that he is not wandering in a trackless world without one to direct him. Further, he is assured that a glorious reception is planned for him when he arrives at his destination. No Christian of any experience will question the fact that God's guidance is often by strange ways, which at times are most perplexing. In fact there are occasions when it appears that no progress is being made at all, but that one is going in circles. At such times, it is helpful to realise that other saints have known this experience, and have put on record their convictions. For example in the poem by A. B. Grosart entitled, 'He leads round', in one verse he expresses it thus:

> *He leads round, but He leads right,*
> *Heaviest burden groweth light:*
> *Marah! Elim! Wilderness!*
> *Each in turn the Lord doth bless;*
> *Canaan shines, far-off but bright;*
> *He leads round, but He leads right.*

It is no small thing to realise that He who made the world, is our guide through it; for sometimes the way is shrouded, as when Jeremiah cried in Lamentations 3:2, *'He hath led me, and brought me into darkness, but not into light'*. From this, and other passages, we learn that God does sometimes bring His people into the dark; but from many other scriptures we are assured that they are not left there. Jeremiah in verse 6 of the same chapter goes further, and says, *'He hath set me in dark places. . . .'* What then is to be the resort of the believer in such trying circumstances? We may find our answer in Isaiah 50, v. 10, *'Who is among you that feareth the Lord, that obeyeth the voice of His servant, that walketh in darkness*

45

*and hath no light? Let him trust in the name of the Lord, and
stay upon his God.'* One wrote many years ago:

> *The way seems dark about me—overhead*
> *The clouds have long since met in gloomy spread*
> *And, when I looked to see the day break through,*
> *Cloud after cloud came up with volume new.*

If then you feel like him, the answer to such conditions
is to trust in the Lord. There is nothing else that can
be done which will give real help. After all, we know
that it is only we who are in the dark, He who is our
guide has not lost sight of us, nor of the road we travel;
both we, and the way, are in clear view to Him.

> *Though dark be my way,*
> *Since He is my Guide,*
> *'Tis mine to obey,*
> *'Tis His to provide.*
> J. Newton

Look up on a dark night into the sky and note the
innumerable multitude of the starry hosts. Then listen
to God's challenging words to Job, *'Canst thou guide
Arcturus with his sons?'* (38:32). Such words as these,
while they cut man down to size, also give comfort, for

> *He who rolls the stars along,*
> *Speaks all the promises,*

These promises include such words as these, *'I will
guide thee with mine eye,'* (Psalm 32:8); and, *'the Lord
shall guide thee continually* . . . (Isaiah 58:11). Of course
it is blessedly true that He *'leadeth me beside the still
waters,'* and *'in the paths of righteousness'* (Psalm 23). The
prayers of the saints also express the longing for
guidance, as in Psalm 31:3, *'For Thy Name's sake lead
me, and guide me.'*

How blessed is he whose faith is steadfast, relying on
the fact that the Lord has undertaken to bring His
people to glory. True, the possibility of ever reaching
the blessed land of the redeemed, at times seems in the

balance. We are bewildered, and beset with obstacles great and small. It is easy to sing

> *I'd rather walk in the dark with God*
> *Than go alone in the light,*
>
> M. J. Brainerd

but not so easy with a restful heart to do it. Yet still the exhortation stands, '*Be not afraid, only believe*'. (Mark 5 : 36). The disciples were fearful as they struggled to cross the lake in the dark and stormy night. But Jesus came, just at the darkest hour.

> *Under the wildest night, the heaviest woe,*
> *When earth looks desolate—heaven dark with doom,*
> *Faith has a fire-flash of the heart to show*
> *The face of the Eternal in the gloom.*
>
> G. Massey

Was not Christ justified in asking the disciples, 'Where is your faith?' and are we not justified in believing that God's promise of guidance is our assurance of safe arrival. So may our prayer ever be,

> *Guide me, O thou great Jehovah,*
> *Pilgrim through this barren land. . .*

And may we rest in the knowledge that He is our Guide, and thus be comforted of God.

# THE COMFORT OF GOD'S PROVIDENCE

*'And Abraham said, My son, God will provide Himself a lamb for a burnt offering. . . .'*

Genesis 22 : 8.

This is the first time the word 'provide' appears in the Scriptures, and it is not without significance that it relates to sacrifice; and the only sacrifice acceptable to God is that which He Himself provides.

It is also a fact that the word, 'Providence' occurs only once in the Bible, in Acts 24 : 2, and there it is used by Paul in relation to Felix, and the benefits he had bestowed upon the people. In spite of this, we have very clear evidences of the fact that God's provision is both universal and particular.

> *Say not, my soul, from whence*
> *Shall God relieve thy care;*
> *Remember, Omnipotence hath servants everywhere.*

Statements to the effect that all such provision is indeed of God, can be deduced from David's utterance in 1 Chronicles 29 : 14, *'for all things come of Thee, and of Thine own have we given Thee'.*

In nature, we see God as the provider of all things. *'Thou visitest the earth, and waterest it: Thou greatly enrichest it with the river of God, which is full of water: Thou preparest them corn, when Thou hast so provided for it.'* (Psalm 65 : 9).

The provision made for Elijah and others too numerous to mention, could be cited as further evidence of God's providential care.

> *O Lord, how happy should we be,*
> *If we could cast our care on Thee,*
> *If we from self could rest;*
> *And feel at heart that One above,*
> *In perfect wisdom, perfect love,*
> *Is working for the best.*
> J. Anstice.

49

East Hagbourne, Berkshire

The hand of God in providence is ceaselessly working. There is never any cessation of His activity, nor any power that can thwart His purposes. Further, His resources are infinite. Once this fact is grasped, we have no difficulty in understanding Paul's words, '*My God shall supply all your need, according to His riches in glory by Christ Jesus.*' (Philippians 4:19).

True, the ways of Providence are past finding out, so that in the words of Mavor, 'How often is Providence as kind in what it denies as in what it grants!' Again, experience shows that those things which seem to be against us, are in reality working for our good. 'While Pharaoh builds his treasure-cities, he is unconsciously working his own ruin. While Israel totters on the margin of a yawning gulf, Moses is born.' (Oosterzee).

God indeed, as Cowper sings

> . . . *moves in a mysterious way*
> *His wonders to perform.*

Yes, God moves, but oh how slow sometimes His movements appear to us. The incident concerning Mary and Martha, when they had to wait for Christ's coming, teaches us, that though His movements may seem so tardy as to be too late, they never are. Martha's utterance in John 11:21, 'Lord, if Thou hadst been here, my brother had not died,' is an illustration of this. The sequel to her utterance, when Lazarus came forth from the tomb, is a very forceful lesson that we must

> *Judge not the Lord by feeble sense,*
> *But trust Him for His grace;*
> *Behind a frowning providence*
> *He hides a smiling face.*

As God provided for Abraham on Mount Moriah, so He has provided for us on Calvary. Full provision is made there to meet all the sinner's need. '*He that spared not His own Son, but delivered Him up for us all, how shall He not with Him also freely give us all things.*' (Romans 8:32).

To live by the day in dependence upon an All-wise Providence, is to live well.

*"Day by day the manna fell;*
*Oh, to learn this lesson well!*
*Still, by constant mercy fed,*
*Give me, Lord, my daily bread."*

It is good and necessary always to remember that God orders men's ways, ordains the conditions and circumstances of life, directs all events, and is in full control of all matters great and small. When life seems to be in utter confusion, and the perplexities of our condition baffle our understanding; when we feel like one of an earlier age who wrote:

*Perplexities do throng upon my sight,*
*Like scudding fog-banks, to obscure the light;*
*Some new dilemma rises every day*
*And I can only shut my eyes and pray.*

Many weary ones have struggled on, month after month, seeing no purpose in God's dealings with them, and have 'wondered where the scene would end'. The disciples, too, when Christ was with them, were often puzzled by His actions; on one occasion Jesus said to Peter, '*What I do thou knowest not now, but thou shalt know hereafter.*' (John 13:7). The blessed fact remains though, that, as is said of Him, 'He Himself knew what He would do.' He always does, and consequently God never has to improvise.

The providence of God is working all things for the good of His people always. Nothing comes unsent, or unseen, into the life of the believer, which means he can take his stand with John Newton and sing:

*Since all that I meet shall work for my good*
*The bitter is sweet, the medicine is food;*
*Though painful at present, 'twill cease before long,*
*And then O how pleasant the conqueror's song.*

He therefore who relies on the Divine providence will be comforted of God.

# THE COMFORT OF
# GOD'S FAITHFULNESS

*'Great is Thy Faithfulness.'*

Lamentations 3 : 23

In order that we may condition our hearts and minds to this theme and its implications, let us note three passages of Scripture. The first is a dogmatic statement in 1 Corinthians 1 : 9. *'God is faithful. . . .'* He therefore can never be unfaithful. This is a great comfort for we note, too, that this word is repeated in 1 Corinthians 10 : 13 in relation to temptation.

The second passage is in Psalm 36 : 5, *'Thy faithfulness reacheth unto the clouds.'* Here is the suggestion of unbounded faithfulness. The third passage indicates the continuity of His faithfulness, for in Psalm 119 : 90, we read, 'Thy faithfulness is unto all generations.'

This whole blessed truth is of the utmost importance to the believer, for on the faithfulness of God our salvation depends. How humbling a thought it is that God should ever remain faithful to such unfaithful ones as us. Yet Paul rejoiced in the great fact expressed in 1 Thessalonians 5 : 24, *'Faithful is He that calleth you, Who also will do it.'* Do what? For answer, read the previous verse, and it will be seen that the preservation of spirit, soul and body are referred to; and He who called, will be faithful to complete what He has begun. Thus we deduce that our salvation depends not upon what we are, but upon what He is.

Daily the Christian is aware of the faithlessness of his own heart, and of the fact that 'others faithless prove'.

*Thou art my pilot wise,*
*My compass is Thy Word;*
*My soul each storm defies*
*While I have such a Lord!*
*I trust Thy faithfulness and power*
*To save me in the trying hour.*

Glen Coe, Argyllshire

To every saint there come the times of testing, when faith is sorely tried and when afflictions bear heavily upon the spirit. If these afflictions bring questionings and doubts to the soul, let us not imagine that they are without any purpose. The Psalmist says *'Before I was afflicted I went astray,'* (Psalm 119:67); then in verse 71 he declares, *'It is good for me that I have been afflicted'*; and in verse 75 states, *'. . . Thou in faithfulness hast afflicted me. . . .'*

A Scottish minister, visiting a Christian woman, said to her, 'Supposing after all, God were to let you drop into hell!' 'Even as He likes,' was her reply. 'But if He does, He will lose more than I do.' This was a true witness. God cannot break His word. She relied upon the faithfulness of God.

> *"Praise Him for His grace and favour*
> *To our fathers in distress;*
> *Praise Him still the same as ever,*
> *Slow to chide, and swift to bless*
> *Praise Him! Praise Him!*
> *Glorious in His faithfulness."*

The faithfulness of God is a bulwark in every age, both to the individual and to the church universal. The believer can be assured that God never has been, nor ever will be faithless to any who trust in Him. That would be contrary to His nature.

Sadly we reflect upon the faithlessness of our own hearts; and the awareness of this causes deep distress. Satan is not slow to suggest that seeing we have been so faithless, we can hardly expect God to remain faithful. Over against Satan's suggestion, we put Paul's words to Timothy, 'If we believe not, yet He abideth faithful: He cannot deny Himself.' What a comfort to remember this, and to know that He understands when faith is low, and fears are high. When in those hours of gloom and despair, we cry out of the darkness to Him, He will hear our prayer.

*In the spaces of the night,*
*In the depths of dim affright,*
*Jesus, with our trials tried,*
*Do not Thou forsake my side!*
*Childlike on Thy faithful breast*
*Hold my heart and bid me rest.*
F. T. Palgrave

To know we have a faithful Friend who will 'never leave us nor forsake us,' but with an unchanging love, will care for us, and strengthen us in our times of weakness, is to know a truth which is insisted upon in the Scripture. In the last book of the Bible, Chapter 19:11, Jesus Christ is called *'Faithful and True'*. What a glorious description, and how comforting to know that it is an accurate statement. John Milton enshrined this truth in his hymn,

*Let us with a gladsome mind*
*Praise the Lord for He is kind;*
*For His mercies shall endure,*
*Ever faithful, ever sure.*

The ages roll on, continually revealing the sombre fact that neither men, nor men's words, can be relied upon. But the passing years also bear eloquent testimony to the faithfulness of God. Therefore, fear not believer, for in this divinely revealed truth that, 'God is faithful,' you have solid ground for confidence. It is a guarantee of your security, enabling you to say

*I trust Thy faithfulness and power*
*To save me in the trying hour.*

May you in pondering the greatness of His faithfulness be comforted of God.

# THE COMFORT OF GOD'S PEACE

*'Peace I leave with you, my peace I give unto you: not as the world giveth give I unto you. Let not your heart be troubled, neither let it be afraid.'*

John 14:27.

Surely these are amongst the most beautiful utterances of the Lord Jesus, and have brought quietness to many a troubled heart.

> *Happy are they that learn, in Thee,*
> *Though patient suffering teach,*
> *The secret of enduring strength,*
> *And praise too deep for speech—*
> *Peace that no presence from without,*
> *No strife within can reach.*
>
> A. L. Waring

But how many of us can say we have attained to such a standard? Restfulness and serenity are sought after, and longed for, by men and women everywhere, but are seldom found. It is salutary therefore, to remind ourselves from the Word of God that, *'There is no peace, saith my God, to the wicked.'* (Isaiah 57:21). It is essential in view of this, that we should examine our relationship to God. If we are not reconciled unto God by the death of His Son, we cannot possibly have any understanding of true peace, for this is something which can only be known by those who have been 'redeemed by the precious blood of Christ'. This is the first thing; for we read that Christ 'made peace through the blood of His cross. . . .' Consequently, if there is no saving knowledge of Jesus Christ, it is impossible that the peace of which He speaks can be known. But assuming that we have been brought to repentance, confession, and assurance of salvation, then we enter into the heritage of peace spoken of by Christ.

> *"Peace, perfect peace, in this dark world of sin?*
> *The blood of Jesus whispers peace within."*

57

Muckross Lake, Killarney

This is a blessed experience, but we must also recognise that there are powers ever seeking to disturb the peace. The world, the flesh, and the Devil, are implacable enemies, and the Christian has to contend with them as he journeys on to his eternal home. Let none under-estimate the reality of these foes. Their activity is constant and intense, and they often succeed in creating disturbances in the hearts of God's people. Well might Charlotte Elliott write:

> *Christian seek not yet repose,*
> *Cast thy dreams of ease away,*
> *Thou art in the midst of foes:*
> *'Watch and pray.'*

Nevertheless, let us not exalt the powers that be against us, to a higher position in our thinking than the powers that be for us. While it is true that we '. . . *wrestle against principalities, against powers, against the rulers of the darkness of this world, against spiritual wickedness in high places,'* (Ephesians 6:12), it is also true that these are not the supreme powers. Satan is indeed described as the *'prince of the power of the air'*; (Ephesians 2:2), but Jesus Christ is described as *'King of Kings, and Lord of Lords,'* (Revelation 19:16); and it is into His hands that all power is committed. Both the Old Testament and the New, speak frequently of peace as coming from God; as for example in Isaiah 26:3, *'Thou wilt keep him in perfect peace, whose mind is stayed on Thee, because he trusteth in Thee'*; and in that well loved passage in Philippians 4:6, 7, *'Be careful for nothing; but in everything by prayer and supplication with thanksgiving let your requests be made known unto God. And the peace of God, which passeth all understanding, shall keep your hearts and minds through Christ Jesus'*. See the Prince of Peace in action on the stormy sea, when He said, 'Peace, be still,'

> *"The wild winds hushed; the angry deep*
> *Sank, like a little child to sleep;*
> *The sullen billows ceased to leap,*
> *At Thy will."*

What a tremendous and comforting truth Elihu uttered when he declared, in Job 34:29, '*When He giveth quietness, who then can make trouble?*'

The peace of God in the soul is something rich and deep, keeping the soul steadfast, for 'He is our peace'; so that

> *When mighty sea-winds madly blow,*
> *And tear the scattered waves,*
> *Peaceful as summer woods, below*
> *Lie darkling ocean caves:*
> *The wind of words may toss my heart,*
> *But what is that to me!*
> *'Tis but a surface storm—Thou art*
> *My deep, still, resting sea.*
>
> G. Macdonald

In this restless world, with our restless hearts, how we need to know more of God's peace within; and how thankful we should be that He has given so many gracious words of comfort concerning His peace. Travelling on the turbulent seas of life, often fearful and apprehensive, we need to remember that our Lord and Master is He who, 'walketh on the water, and commandeth, Peace be still'. He can give peace to the heart assailed by the storms of sin, because He can by His blessed Spirit assure us that

> *Though on earth we've scorn and trouble,*
> *In ourselves but shame and sin;*
> *All without the reign of darkness,*
> *Fearful conflict oft within;*
> *He who died and lives for ever,*
> *Saves and guards from every ill;*
> *Jesus walks upon the waters,*
> *And commandeth, 'Peace be still!'*
>
> Ellerton

May He so speak to us that we shall know the comfort of His peace.

# THE COMFORT OF GOD'S HOME

*'Whilst we are at home in the body, we are absent from the Lord
. . . we are . . . willing rather to be absent from the body, and to be
present with the Lord.'*

2 Corinthians 5 : 6–8.

*'I go to prepare a place for you.'*

John 14 : 2.

Home! What a lovely word this is, conjuring up
pictures of fellowship and happy family life for so
many. Home is the place where the Father is; and we
cannot but think of Christ's lovely words in John 17 : 24,
*'Father, I will that they also, whom Thou hast given me, be
with me where I am; that they may behold my glory which
Thou hast given me. . . .'* This is the will of Christ for His
people; the hope of attaining to that heavenly home
above. Let us not lose the comfort of this hope, by
failing to think about it sometimes.

We often, and rightly, think of ourselves as strangers
and pilgrims in the earth, but

> *Ye are travelling home to God*
> *In the way the fathers trod;*
> *They are happy now, and ye*
> *Soon their happiness shall see.*
> J. Cennick

Are these only vague, pious, but utterly unrealistic
ideals and hopes? Then discard your Bible, for it has
much to say about the blessed future of the saints; if
this is untrue, how can we rely upon its other statements? If Christ said, 'I go to prepare a place for you,'
as we believe He did, then let us derive the maximum
comfort from a consideration of it. It is a heavenly
home, a place of love, joy, peace and perfect service. In
our present state, conditioned as we are to sin, pain,
sorrow, tears, and death, we find it hard to visualise a
home where there is no possibility of these things
entering in. Let us not, however, because of our limited

61

Arkesden, Essex

capacities, and oft-times weak faith, limit God, for :

> *"If God has made this world so fair*
> *Where sin and death abound;*
> *How beautiful, beyond compare*
> *Will paradise be found."*

If we have 'Christ in us, the hope of glory,' then we can, and should, with joyful anticipation, look forward to that time when He will bring us Home to glory. After all, the days and years are fast slipping away, and at times

> *"One sweetly solemn thought*
> *Comes to me o'er and o'er—*
> *I'm nearer home today*
> *Than I ever have been before."*

Our hymnology is full of references to our heavenly home, together with clear indications of our right to enter into it. Isaac Watts, when he contemplated the blessedness of those there, wrote :

> *I asked them whence their victory came,*
> *They, with united breath,*
> *Ascribed their conquest to the Lamb,*
> *Their triumph to His death.*

Paul expressed his *'desire to depart, and to be with Christ . . . '* (Philippians 1:23). Abraham we read, *'looked for a city which hath foundations, whose builder and maker is God.'* (Hebrews 11:10). We, too, would subscribe to this, for we read again in Hebrews 13:14, *'. . . here have we no continuing city, but we seek one to come.'*

When we reflect upon Christ's words, 'In my Father's House are many mansions . . .', we can but dimly and very imperfectly visualise the prospect before us. Yet He surely meant what He said; and there have been saints, who like Montgomery have exclaimed

> *My Father's house on high,*
> *Home of my soul, how near*
> *At times, to faith's far-seeing eye,*
> *Thy golden gates appear.*

Picture language, do you say? Then surely the reality will not be less wonderful than the picture. Paul declares in 1 Corinthians 2 : 9, '*Eye hath not seen, nor ear heard, neither have entered into the heart of man, the things which God hath prepared for them that love Him.*' Does not such an utterance thrill your heart, and lift your Spirit? Is it not stimulating to know that He who purchased your salvation by His own blood, gives such assurance of future blessedness? Be comforted, in anticipation of what is sure, because Christ has promised that He will come again to take His people home. Let us sing in prospect:

> *Oh sweet and blessèd country,*
> *The home of God's elect!*
> *Oh sweet and blessèd country,*
> *That eager hearts expect!*
> *Jesus, in mercy bring us*
> *To that dear land of rest,*
> *Who art with God the Father,*
> *And Spirit, ever blest!*
> (Trans. J. M. Neale)

Look from this dark world of sin and woe, to that land of purity and joy, and rejoice in the comfort given to the saints of God that they have a home to go to, when they shall

> *See him face to face,*
> *And sing the story*
> *Saved by grace.*

Then and there, will they indeed be comforted of God in the presence of God—Home at last, and for ever.